Counting the Days,

Lighting the Candles

By

Elyse M. Fitzpatrick

&

Jessica L. Thompson

With Jami Nato

TABLE OF CONTENTS

Counting the Days, Lighting the Candles

An Advent Devotional

We love the Christmas season…mostly. We say "mostly" because, like you, we get caught up in trying to make it special, forgetting what makes it special: the birth of the Son of God, Jesus Christ; hence, the reason for this little advent devotional.

A Few Words Before We Begin

You can choose to use this devotional any way you like. Let it serve you and your family; please don't serve it. We don't want you to end up resenting it or feeling enslaved to it or guilty if you don't get it done. There won't be any rules here, just suggestions about how to utilize this celebration in your family's life.

We can just see it now: a mom, in the middle of reading the devotional, yells at her children, "Stop talking!! I'm trying to read to you about Jesus! Don't you know that Jesus is the reason for the season?! Stop asking about presents! If you don't sit still you won't get any! And, Johnnie, put the lighter down and stop trying to light your sister's hair on fire!"

Above all, please don't make this a way to earn righteousness or "make a tradition" that will somehow save your children when they, like you, are "prone to wander." Traditions don't save us, the Christ-child does.

We have also linked to a product on Amazon that you may or may not like. Use it, don't use it, make it your own, use the traditional colors of the candles (purple, pink, white), or not. Or don't use candles at all. Or dig through a drawer until you find leftover sparkly birthday candles and stick them in pancakes. Some women like to be domestic goddesses. That's great. (It's not where our gifts lie and we're trying not to be jealous of you.)

We've also included a series of suggested activities for those of you who would enjoy this with your children. These projects weren't created by us! (Giant surprise, we know!)

They were created by our friend, Jami Nato, the Craftelangelo of the Tactile-Sensory-How-Did-She-Think-Of-That World. If you decide to do them, may you be blessed with children who won't 1) eat paste instead of their pancakes, 2) glue their eyelids shut, 3) color on the Christmas Hymnal that has somehow survived all 52 other children in your lineage and is now being destroyed by your family (Sorry about that, great-great grandma!), and 4) play barbershop while you're looking for matches.

The point of all this: to enjoy this event, to enjoy your children. The child Jesus didn't color in the lines perfectly either. Enjoy Him. He's here for you.

The Tradition

Traditionally, Advent Calendars have five candles on an evergreen wreath (three purple, one pink, and one white candle.)

- The first candle is the **Prophecy** Candle. This candle represents **hope or expectation in anticipation of the coming Messiah.**

- The second candle, purple, is the **Bethlehem** Candle. This candle represents **love and Christ's birth.**

- The third candle, pink, is the **Shepherd's** Candle, representing **joy.**

- The fourth candle, purple, is the **Angel's** Candle. This candle represents **peace.**

- Finally, on Christmas Eve, the white candle--the **Christ** candle--is lit. It represents the light of the life of Christ that has come into the world. The white represents Christ's purity, for although He was tempted in all ways as we are, He is the only one without sin. Christ is the sinless Savior, and, because of His unparalleled love and life, those who trust Him by faith are forgiven for their sins and are made whiter than snow.

- The Evergreen Wreath representing **eternal life.**

Like we said before, use this devotional in any way you like, and don't worry if you don't get this done every day or in the right order. We tell you not to worry because you're not the one bringing Christ to your children. The Holy Spirit does that. Of course, He may use you as means to accomplish His work…or He may not. You can pray and then trust that He will use this season and your entire life in just the way He chooses.

You may want to do this devotional every day beginning on December 1, or you may just have time to do it every Sunday in December…or Tuesdays if that works better. If your children are able to listen, you might want to read the entire passage for each day aloud. Or you can just read it to yourself. The point is for you to relax, rest, and most of all, rejoice.

We've included readings for parents and readings for children. Some of your older children may want to hear both readings, while your toddlers will probably just enjoy the fact that mama is lighting a candle.

A word from Jami

For these activities during advent, we suggest that you pick one night of the week without a lot of events. For instance, in our family, Tuesday nights are soccer practice nights, my husband often works nights, I'm rushed to get dinner to the table and often end up with flames coming out of my eyes by 6pm. Thus, advent activities shall not happen on Tuesdays. Acknowledge your limitations and plan accordingly.

Our second suggestion is: Plan ahead just a bit. Try to pick the same night every week, then as silly as it sounds, write it on your calendar. That morning, gather your supplies. For me, when I read, "that morning," it usually means, "20 minutes before the activity." And that's ok, too. See above where I discuss acknowledging limitations. You will notice that there are no advent activities the last week of this devotional. This is intentional, as it will likely already be filled with many activities and events. Please enjoy the time together with your family!

The third suggestion: Limit distractions. Put those smart phones in the fireplace and watch them turn into colorful sparks as you tell stories around the fire. Ok, maybe just stick them in the other room? Putting the distractions away says that this time together is important. It is difficult to focus during the holidays anyway, so keeping some time set apart for focused interaction with God's word and each other is needed and beneficial.

And so we begin, counting the days,

and lighting the candles...

December 1 [i]

- Light the first (purple) candle (the Prophecy Candle), which represents hope or expectation in anticipation of the coming Messiah

  Read: Psalm 113

Thoughts for Parents:

It is right to begin this season of advent by saying:

"Praise the Lord!...From the rising of the sun to its setting, the name of the Lord is to be praised!"[ii]

Yes, of course we know that we should praise the Lord. We know that He is good and that He deserves our worship, but sometimes we find it difficult to get there. And then, when we discover that coldness in our souls, we wonder whether He still loves us at all, which results in a complete dearth of heartfelt praise.

Here's the good news from our reading: "The Lord is high above all nations, and His glory is above the heavens!" Yes, He "sits on high" but He also looks far down on the "heavens and the earth." He "raises the poor from the dust and lifts the needy from the ash heap." You see, the good news is that God isn't only transcendent and sovereign. No, not at all. The good news is that He's also imminent—He's with you right there, right where you are, right now. How do we know? We know because of Christmas; God the Son came to earth as Jesus the Man for one primary reason: to raise the poor from the dust and rescue the needy from the trash. *Rejoice!* He came for you and your family, no matter how lowly, how insignificant, or how much you struggle. He sees your poverty and your neediness, and He's come to answer it all.

Thoughts for Children:

Do you ever feel like God is far away from you? Or like He is so big and powerful that He would never notice a little child like you? Our verses today in Psalm 113 talk about that very thing. You see, God is big and powerful. Our verses say, "He is seated on high." Imagine some one in a very big throne looking down on everybody else, thinking important thoughts, and doing important things. You probably think that someone so important doesn't care about unimportant, little kids; but, you see, our God is different. Our verses say that God takes the most unimportant people and raises them up to sit with all the princes. *God really does see you. God really does love you.* As we get close to Christmas, we are going to see that God loves us so much that He gave us the best gift possible. He gives gifts to the people that most everybody else wouldn't even bother with. God gives gifts to us because He loves us, not because we are big and powerful.

December 2

Read: 2 Peter 3:8-10

Thoughts for Parents:

Many people in Christ's day didn't recognize His coming, but that didn't stop Him from loving them and saving them. And many people today don't recognize Him either, but that doesn't stop Him from being patient and waiting for their salvation to be complete. The Lord may return while you're reading this or He may not return until after you're long gone. We don't know when He's coming back but we do know that He's not hesitating because He's angry. No, He's hesitating because He's "not wishing that any should perish, but that all should reach repentance."

Jesus' contemporaries were waiting, too. They were waiting for the Messiah, for the One to come who would set them free and save them. Even though many did not recognize Him, when He came, He still marched on from Bethlehem toward Calvary and their salvation.

In this passage, you *are* the "beloved" of God, those whom He has chosen and loved. Yet, there are still other "beloveds" who have yet to come to Him, perhaps even members of your family. Don't be anxious, because He's not. He's waiting because He loves sinners. In the end, in eternity you'll see that everything came together just when and as it should have. Everything wrong will be made right. Everything sad will be made joyous.

Thoughts for Children:

Waiting is very hard, especially when you are waiting for something that you really want. We have 23 days until we celebrate Christmas, and every day feels like a thousand years. In our verses today we hear about what God is waiting for; He is waiting to come again. Jesus already came once a very long time ago; He came as a baby and that is what we celebrate at Christmas time. He came because He loves us. He wanted to make a way for us to be a part of His family. He came because He knew we were all *sinners*, which is just a fancy way of saying that He knows we don't obey the way we should or love the way we should. The terrible thing about sin is wherever sin goes tears follow. He came because we wanted us to *repent*, which is just a fancy way of saying that we need to say we are sorry for all the unkind things we have done.

The day He comes back again will be the day that all sad things will become unsad. Everything that is wrong will become right. All the tears and all the sin will be gone. Every day we wait for Christmas day, we remember how Jesus is waiting to come back one more time. The reason He is waiting is because He wants lots and lots of people to repent and become a part of His forever family. You can become part of His forever family today. You don't have to wait. All you have to do is believe that He loves you even though you disobey.

December 3

Read: Genesis 3:15

Thoughts for Parents:

Everything had gone terribly wrong. The beautiful paradise was ruined. Their sweet transparency and vulnerability and intimacy was shattered. For the first time Adam and Eve knew shame, embarrassment, and humiliation. They were lost from each other, from their Lord and from the promise of a blessed life. They hid. They tried to cover themselves up from the judgment that they knew was coming; they tried to make themselves presentable. And even though they were judged and the curse of death for disobedience was placed upon them and all their children, they didn't get what they truly deserved. No, instead of death they were given a promise: A promise that all their folly would be placed upon a Man--a descendant of Eve the Sinner--who would be bruised in their place, but who would crush their enemy beneath His heel. Salvation would come; a baby would be born from "her offspring"--Mary, Eve's descendant would labor and give birth in humiliation, shame, and isolation—and this baby would be a Conqueror and would forever triumph over the wicked one who delighted in destroying the beauty the Lord He hated had loved. This descendant would crush the enemy through shame, humiliation and isolation, by hanging on a cross, alone. We can trust that the Lord will fulfill all His promises to save us even when we feel lost, ashamed, and humiliated. He never forgets His word; He never breaks a promise. He is victorious in all He does.

Thoughts for Children:

In the very beginning, Adam and Eve sinned. They decided that what they wanted was more important than what God wanted. The reason God gives us rules is because He loves us and He know what is the best way for us to be happy. He wanted Adam and Eve to be happy, but they didn't trust His love or believe that He wanted them to be happy. Satan, who was disguised as a serpent, told Adam and Eve that they couldn't trust God. They chose to try and make themselves happy instead of obeying what God told them.

Any time we disobey God's rules it is because we don't believe He loves us enough and we don't trust that His heart is for us. Like we talked about yesterday, whenever we sin tears always follow. Sadness and sin always go together.

The exciting part about God is He doesn't leave us in our sadness. He makes a way for us to be happy again. He did that for Adam and Eve on that very day they disobeyed Him. He promised them that He would send a warrior to come and kill the serpent. He promised them that He would win the war. And even though sometimes it looks like sadness might win, we know God always keeps His promises. Jesus was the warrior that came to beat the serpent. The day He was born was the day that Satan's defeat became a reality.

December 4

> **Read**: Genesis 12:1-3, 7

Thoughts for Parents:

Yesterday we read that God promised to crush the head of the serpent, our enemy, Satan, through the weakness of a Man born to a weak, shamed woman. Today we see the Lord reiterating this promise of blessing to another flawed person, a man named Abraham and his flawed wife, Sarah. God promised that through one of Abraham's descendants, He would bring blessing on the whole world. But this promise of blessing to the whole earth wasn't fulfilled in Isaac or Jacob. No, these sons weren't the ones who would bring the blessing. The Apostle Paul applies the promise of blessing to Jesus,

> Now the promises were made to Abraham and to his offspring. It does not say, "And to offsprings," referring to many, but referring to one, "And to your offspring," who is Christ (Galatians 3:16).

In his sermon on the Day of Pentecost, Peter identified Jesus as the one who would bring the promised blessing,

You are the sons of the prophets and of the covenant that God made with your fathers, saying to Abraham, "And in your offspring shall all the families of the earth be blessed." God having raised up his servant, sent him to you first, to bless you by turning every one of you from your wickedness (Acts 3:25-26).

Jesus, the One born in a manger, is no mere infant of questionable lineage. He's a conqueror who will bring blessing to millions, to Jews and to Gentiles. He doesn't do this by making us wealthy or giving us our perfect life now. He does this by turning our hearts toward Him and away from our sin. He gives us faith to believe in His promise and He proves that He is trustworthy by living and dying in our place. He makes us believe that He is that good and that loving. He is the promised blessing.

Thoughts for Children:

If you were going to pick a person to be your most important warrior in a battle, who would you choose? You would probably choose the person from the most powerful family with the strongest mom and dad. You would probably choose the richest person who could buy the best weapons. You would probably choose someone who was very popular so that everybody would want to be on his side. Well, that is not how God chose who was going to be His most important warrior. Just like we read yesterday, God promised another group of people that He was going to send someone to be the Conqueror of Satan. In the Old Testament, God promises over and over again that He is getting ready to send someone. And just like you are waiting for Christmas Day, the people in the Bible kept waiting and waiting for the conqueror to come. God didn't choose His warrior from the strongest or the richest or the most popular family. God chose His warrior from a family that nobody knew. God didn't promise to send a conqueror because the people that needed rescuing were good and kind. God sent a conqueror because the people that needed rescuing were weak and couldn't fight on their own.

Actually He sent a warrior to the very people that were fighting against Him. He wanted to help and take care of the people who were His enemies, the people that disobeyed Him. God acted in this way because He is the most loving and the most kind; God does this to show us His love and His power. God gives to us because He loves to bless His people. He loves to take care of His forever family. The conqueror that was promised was Jesus. And Christmas Day, the day you are waiting for, was the exact same day all the people in the Bible were waiting for too, the day that Jesus the conqueror would be born.

December 5

Read: Isaiah 7:14 and Matthew 1:23

Thoughts for Parents:

Is there any sweeter name by which to call Jesus than Immanuel? He is God *with* us. Our familiarity with this name has numbed our senses to the shocking nature of what it means. Say it out loud to yourself right now, "God with us." This name is the answer to the question who is Jesus. His name is Immanuel. By very nature God, Jesus became completely man so that He could be with us. He is with us in every sense of the word. In the movie *My Blue Heaven*[iii], Steve Martin has a line that he repeats over and over again, "I'm with you. When I say I'm with you I don't mean I understand where you're coming from. I mean, I'm with you." When Mary conceived Jesus by the work of the Holy Spirit, this was God's enduring proclamation that He was with us. Jesus becomes one of us so that He could relate to us in every way. He was tempted as we are "yet without sin," He knew how to "refuse the evil and choose the good."

In every area where we choose the evil and refuse the good, Jesus continues to say He is God with us. How is this possible? It is only possible by the work of God. He initiates the relationship by sending Jesus to be with us, and then He pursues this relationship by breaking down every barrier. This pursuing is seen Matthew 1:21, "She will bear a son, and you shall call his name Jesus, for he will save his people from their sins." God is with us with the purpose of saving us from our sin. Every day He chose good and refused evil so that we could be saved from our sin. Every excruciating moment of temptation that He faced was to assure us that He knows our lives, that He understands our trials, and that He is with us.

Thoughts for Children:

Back in the olden days your name meant a lot. It wasn't just something your mom or dad yelled when she wanted you to clean up your room. Your name actually had to do with who you were. Jesus' name is very important. Jesus was called Immanuel, which means "God with us." Do you every feel like you are alone? Do you ever feel like no one understands you? God named Jesus a very special name to remind you that you aren't alone...ever. God sent Jesus to earth to make sure we know for a fact that we aren't alone.

During Christmas, we talk a lot about how Jesus was a baby, but have you every thought about the fact that He was also a child. He was a young person, just like you. He had to learn how to read and write and talk and walk just like you. He had friends that did unkind things, He had to share His toys, and He had to obey His parents, just like you.

The big difference between you and Jesus, though, is that He always chose the right way to act. He did this so that He could make the second part of His name come true. He was called Jesus because that meant, "he would save people from their sin." So, every time you choose to do the wrong thing instead of the right thing, you can remember this part of His name: He came to save you from your sin. He came to live the life you couldn't ever live no matter how hard you try. He also came to take all the punishment for all of the times you disobeyed and for all the times you will disobey in the future. He came so that you would know you are never alone. He is God with you all the time.

December 6

Read: Isaiah 9:6-7 and Matthew 1:18-25; 4:16

Thoughts for Parents:

Today, many parents are aware of the gender of their child before he or she is even born, and, consequently, they have the privilege of picking out a name before birth. In our passage today, we're introduced to our Savior, but His name is something so much more than just a name. His name not only tells us what to call Him, it also tells us what He's been sent to do. Consider this: from the time this little baby is born, His destiny is already planned out for Him. He won't be spending His life in obscurity, following in the footsteps of His earthly father.

No, He'll be a wonderful wise counselor, He'll be the mighty God, this baby will be an everlasting Father — although He'll not have any natural children of His own.

And, although He will spend much of His life in conflict, He will be a Prince who brings peace with Him; Peace from His

Father to those in rebellion against Him, peace among men and women who used to fight for preeminence.

As wonderful as all those titles are, the greatest promise of all is this, "And of his government and peace there will be no end." This wonderful baby is establishing a rule of peace that will never end. No matter how bleak things look; no matter how overwhelmed or despairing or faithless you feel today, you can be assured of one thing: there will be no end of His government and peace — not government at war, but government and peace. With His birth in a lowly manger, He's bringing in a whole new kingdom, and nothing will ever stop Him.

Thoughts for Children:

Yesterday we learned what Jesus' name meant. We learned that it meant two different things. Do you remember what they were? His name means God is always with us, and it means that He will take away our sin. Today we will learn all the amazing things that happen because He is with us and He takes away our sin.

The Bible describes Jesus as a Wonderful Counselor. That is just a fancy way of saying that whenever you don't know what to do you can ask Him for help and He *will* help you, always. The bible describes Him as a Mighty God, which means that whenever you are afraid or feel like things are out of control, you know that He is strong and powerful. Another way that our verse talks about Jesus is as an Everlasting Father. This means that you don't ever have to feel alone or like no one is looking out for you, He is your daddy and He will love you, forever.

The very last way Jesus is described is as a Prince of Peace that reminds us that we don't have to worry about what God thinks about us. Because of what Jesus did, there is and will be peace between you and God, now and forever. God will never be angry with you, as long as you believe that you are a sinner and that Jesus is all of these things for you even though you don't deserve it.

December 7

Read: Isaiah 53:7-8; Acts 8:32-33

Thoughts for Parents:

Have you ever felt humiliated? I know that I have...and on more occasions than I would like to remember. We all militate against humiliation...and, yet, the Lord Jesus came to earth for that specific reason: to be humiliated. Of course, He was humiliated on the cross (and we'll get to that), but His entire life was one humiliation after another. Think of it: He was God; He had always existed in the form of God, enjoying all the blessings and privileges of God, and yet here He was learning table manners and language, submitting to flawed parents, putting up with His little brothers and sisters pulling His hair and wrongly accusing Him to His parents. His entire childhood was a childhood of humiliation: His family was poor; they lived under the tyranny of Rome, His dad worked with his hands. No speaking worlds into existence for Him here. No...carving and sawing and hammering were His lot.

He was humiliated in His very existence — but He was most shockingly humiliated in His crucifixion — at the very moment when He should have been exonerated, when He should have been rescued, "justice was denied him." Why? For you and me…so that we could have mercy.

Thoughts for Children:

Have you every gotten in trouble for something you didn't do? It is the worst feeling to have to take the blame for a bad thing that someone else did. I know when that happens to me I do everything I can to let everyone know that I didn't do it and I should not get in trouble for it. It's just not right or fair to get punished when I did nothing wrong. But you see this is exactly what Jesus did for us. Our sin, all the bad things we do, must be punished. Even though our parents or grandparents or teachers may not see all the bad things we do, God does. God the Father and His Son, Jesus, decided that every single bad thing you and I have ever done, Jesus would take the blame for. That is what He did on the cross. He took the blame for all of our sins.

He didn't complain one time about being blamed for our sin, His love for us stopped Him from saying, "This isn't fair!" He did acted this way so that we could know mercy. Mercy means: we don't get what we deserve. He also took our blame so that we could know grace. Grace means: we get good stuff instead of bad.

And, get this! All of the good things that Jesus deserved for always doing the right things are now ours. They belong to us. We are in God's family. All of the punishment that we deserved for all of the bad things we have done, Jesus took the punishment for. We get all the good things Jesus deserved for living perfectly. He loves us that much and He is that good.

Activity Time

Week one: Prophecy

This week, we focused on the prophecy of Christ's birth. We have hope because God always keeps His promises. He said He would come, and Christmas reminds us that He did show up just like He said He would. He came in human flesh as a tiny baby.

```
you're going on a              then look here
scavenger hunt!
first look here:



then look here                 then look here



then look here                 then look here



then look here                 TIME FOR THE PRIZE!
```

For this week's activity, we'll be doing a scavenger hunt, which will remind us that God keeps His promises. He told us that something would happen and sure enough, it happened!

After you read your devotionals, hand your children a piece of paper that tells them where to find the next clue. For instance, look in daddy's shoe, look under the table, look in the kitchen where the Tupperware is, and, when you walk by the trash can, consider emptying it? I'm kidding. Sort of.

At the end of the scavenger hunt leave them with a small gift, a piece of candy, or an outing like going to get ice cream together. If you have older children, consider making the hunt difficult by using riddles. Although you will be tempted to make it so difficult that they can't actually find the prize, remember: although funny, this defeats the purpose.

If your kids are teenagers, you could take the scavenger hunt outside the home. For example, go to the neighbor's house and get your next clue, go to your friend Sara's house and do five jumping jacks to get your clue, etc.

You can use this template here for the hunt if you'd like.

Take a moment at the end to ask simple questions, if you have time:

- How did you know where to find the next piece of paper?

- Why did you believe that the paper was telling the truth?

Link this activity to trust in God: *You trusted that mom put the papers where she said they would be...you believe me because i am trustworthy.* How much more trustworthy is God! He never lies and never fails. He always keeps His promises.

December 8

Light the second (purple) candle (the Bethlehem Candle), which represents love

Read: Psalm 36, Luke 2:1-7

Thoughts for Parents:

Psalm 36 reminds us that even though there is wickedness in this world, God's steadfast love is ruling and overruling even in the middle of it. Evil men and governments seek to destroy God's people, but we are safely hidden in God's steadfast love: it extends to the heavens; He arranges everything for our good and His glory — to accomplish His eternal plan.

Caesar Augustus wanted to know how many people he could tax; he wanted their money. So without any concern for the lives of those in his care, he ordered everyone to return to their family home. It didn't cross his mind that a very young very pregnant woman would have to get to Bethlehem during the last few days of her pregnancy. Why would he care? But...God would keep her.

And He would accomplish His work of salvation and the eventual overthrow of all the wicked kingdoms of the earth through Augustus's selfish edict. The child born of a virgin would come from Bethlehem. How would that happen? Caesar Augustus would be God's pawn.

When it seems as though everything is out of control and that wickedness is running rampant over God's people, we can remember that God is our refuge and that He is working everything out according to plan. We can rest. He is our refuge.

Thoughts for Children:

There are mean people in the world. There are people that do wrong and are selfish. Sometimes we do what is wrong and we are selfish, too. Caesar Augustus was a mean and wicked man. He was the ruler during the time that Jesus was born. He told everyone that they had to go to the town that they were born in so that he could get money from them. If they didn't go to the town that they were born in they would be punished. Mary and Joseph had to go to Bethlehem. I bet they thought it was a terrible inconvenience to travel when Mary was big and pregnant with Jesus. I bet they couldn't see that any good would come out of Mary getting on a donkey and going almost 70 miles because an evil man told them too. What they didn't know is that Caesar wasn't the one that was in charge. Jesus was supposed to be born in Bethlehem because that was what God had told people thousands of years earlier. So you see, God was really in charge. He was working everything out to show how wise and strong He was.

Sometimes things happen in our lives that feel like the bad people are in charge, but God wants you to know that He is always the one who is really the boss. Not only is He strong enough to do everything He wants, He also loves you enough to make everything work out for your good. His never-ending love guides *everything* in your life.

December 9

Read: John 3:16

Thoughts for Parents:

Do you know what white noise is? I used to live near the I-15 freeway, one of the most traveled roads in America. In fact, I lived within one-quarter mile of it, but I never heard it. Think of it, all that traffic, thousands of cars racing up and down the road, so near that if I was in the right spot I could see them go by...and I never heard it. Why? Because it had become white noise to me. It was there, but I never heard it.

Which brings us to John 3:16. When you saw that our reading for today was this familiar verse, did you decide to skip over it? Did you assume you knew it? Probably. Can you quote it? Possibly. Has it become white noise to you so that the only time it even crosses your consciousness is when some guy with a rainbow wig holds up a sign at an NFL game? But these words should never become overly familiar to us. In these words Jesus himself lays out His entire purpose. He reveals God's plan to grant eternal life to those who deserve death for their disobedience. Death for disobedience is what Adam and Eve and all of us have earned. But God's plan is to overcome the promised curse of death for disobedience by granting us eternal life. How can that be done? Will God renege on His promise? Was he just kidding? No, of course not. Out of love he would send His Son, His only Son, into the world, so that we might not perish under this curse of death, but rather so that we would have eternal life with Him.

Eternal life is not a blessing if it means we're separated from God. That's why the eternal life we're given is life in Him, in His Son. This life is a great delight because it means we will be able to rejoice in His love forever. We've been given the promise of blessing for Christ's obedience. This promise is for all who believe; they are not for all who remember to do everything properly…for none of us do. It's a love-promise, an "I do" from God to us so that we can live with Him forever. Are those truths worthy of being relegated to white noise? Hardly.

Thoughts for Children:

Do you know that one of the most famous verses in the Bible is our verse today? It seems like almost everybody knows John 3:16. What most people don't understand is how crazy cool this verse is. We think "oh yes, God loves us" and "oh yes, He sent His son," and we think it is not that important. But, you see, these words in this verse are the very important. God does love us, and not because we are so sweet, lovely, and do everything right, but just because He decided to love us. And God did send His son, His only son, Jesus, to the earth so that we could be a part of His family. All we have to do is believe. You don't even have to believe perfectly, you don't even have to believe all the time; all you have to do is believe that God loves you and that He gave Jesus to you so that we could be saved. The most beautiful part about God's love is that we can't earn it; all we can do is receive it and say, "thank you." When we receive His gift and say, "thank you," we will be forever His children. We will live always with Him and with the rest of His family in the happiest place ever created. We will be with Him in Heaven.

December 10

Read: 1 John 4:9

Thoughts for Parents:

Yesterday we read about God's love from John 3:16. We thought about how that beautiful passage might have become old hat to us. Today, we're going to think more about what God's love is like. Sometimes when we think about love we think of fat babies floating on clouds with arrows meant to pierce the heart…or we think of nice feelings, pretty sunsets, or Valentines. But God's love is not some abstract principle or saccharine sentiment. No, His love is active, fierce, and actually quite shocking. His love is willing to sacrifice the One He loves most for our sake. God demonstrates the quality of His love when He sends His only Son into the world, a Son who is sent to live as our perfect Representative, to die as a sinner, and to be raised as the head of a whole new race of people--people no longer under the curse for disobedience, but people under the blessing for righteousness. Why would He do this? So we might live.

The truth is that God's love is simply beyond our understanding, and, in fact, without the work of the Holy Spirit, we'll never believe that His love is that strong, that generous, that good. It's just too good to be true. It's His love for sinners that the religious people of Jesus' day (and ours) objected to. *Sinners don't deserve God's love*, we think. *They don't deserve to be with Him!* And while it's true that we deserve justice instead of mercy, because He's God He gets to choose those whom it is right for Him to love...and He's chosen to love us and give us eternal life through the work of His Son.

Why would He want to sacrifice like that? Why would He love like this? Because we are His creation and He loves to love us. Is there something more? Should we try to add anything? Although it's tempting to think that adding something to make God's love make sense would be good, it's actually an insult. We're saying that He really isn't capable of unselfish love...and that's an insult.

Thoughts for Children:

Our verse from yesterday and our verse from today are a lot alike. There are actually a bunch of verses in the Bible that say the very same thing over and over again. This is because we forget that God loves us over and over again. We think that we have to be good little boys and girls in order to earn God's love. We think that God could never love us just to love us, but that we must do sweet things to be loveable. But that is not what the Bible says. The Bible tells us again and again that God loves because that is what God is like. He loves us so much that He gives us everything we need in order to know everything about His love. He loves us even when we don't think we want His love. He loves us even when we do ugly things and forget about His love. His love is stronger and bigger than all the bad things we do.

Even mommies and daddies forget God's love. Every single one of us looks for something to make us happy, maybe a new toy or a new bike or a new video game--we cannot wait to see what presents we will get. The one present that will make us the happiest is already ours. God has already given us His love by giving us Jesus. This love will make us happy

forever.

December 11

Read: Romans 1:1-7

Thoughts for Parents:

How does the Holy Spirit refer to you? What does He call you? He calls us those who are loved by God and called to be saints. That's so amazing. How should He refer to us? I know how He should refer to me: Slow to believe, self-seeking, selfish, and stubborn. That's how I should be known by Him. But that's not who I am before Him. No, I'm His beloved. I am called to be among the saints, the holy ones. Again, that's so amazing. How does God love us? By calling us to be among His holy people. But wait, how can it be that I'm now counted among God's holy ones? Is it because I've all of a sudden gotten my act together? No, not at all. I'm now counted as part of that holy family of people because I've been given grace. Simply, grace is God's unmerited favor on us and the way that works in tandem with His love is that He has decided to favor us with a reputation that we don't deserve: a reputation for being holy, for having fulfilled every law our whole life. How did that happen? Is God just pretending? No, all of Christ's righteousness has been transferred to me so that now, because He loves me, because He has given me unearned favor, I'm counted as a saint, a holy person.

Today when you struggle against sin…when you try to do all the things you need to do to make this Christmas season what you hope it will be, and when everything only serves to point out that you're not making the grade, you can remember: when He thinks of you He thinks: loved and holy. You *are* loved, you *are* a saint.

Thoughts for Children:

When you think of yourself what words do you think of? Do you think little brother or older sister or good boy or bad girl? Do you think goal scorer or piano player or just not good at anything? In our verse for today, God describes you and me in two different ways. First He describes us as beloved. Now that isn't a word we use very often anymore. It just means that you are loved. When you think of yourself, remember that you are one that is loved by God. That is pretty exciting news, isn't it?

The other word that God uses to describe you is saint. Now I am pretty sure no one has ever called you a saint before. It is an old fashioned way of saying that you are a person that always does good.

Now if you have been awake for very long today you have probably done something that was bad. Maybe you didn't do it so anybody could see it, but you thought something mean or you ignored someone that needed help or you didn't do what your parents asked you to do, so how could God possibly call you a saint? Listen up, because this is very, very good news: God calls you a saint because of what Jesus did for you. He doesn't call you a saint because anything you have done. Jesus lived always doing what was right. If you believe God loves you even though you don't deserve His love, all of your badness is hidden by Jesus' goodness. So today when you are thinking about how God looks at you, you can know for certain that you are loved and you are a saint.

December 12

Read: 1 John 3:1-3

Thoughts for Parents:

Today we're going to think about God's love again…but this time we're going to think about His adopting love. A lot of people are adopting children now and that's such a good thing. Adoption is such a blessing; I can understand why people adopt children. Sometimes it's because they're unable to have children of their own. Other times it is because they have been given a vision of what it means to grow up in the foster care system or as an orphan in a poor country and they want to rescue children and give them a chance at life. But the astonishing truth is that we read about today is that God, in His great love, has made us His children; this means that we have all the rights, privileges and inheritances of natural born children, all of the blessings His Son earned.

But the passage tells us that we have more than the possibility of adoption: we are actually His children "now."

What that means is that we will not only share in His blessings but also in the glory that it means to be like Him. In the same way that a child bears a family resemblance, a day is coming when we will finally see the One we've been looking for our whole lives and in that moment we will be transformed. Because we have the promise of being part of His family, we can approach Him in confidence and trust that a day is coming when we will bear the family traits: we will have glorified bodies that will never be sick or die, we will be in our nature what He's made us to be in His sight: sinless and whole and just like our Brother, Jesus.

Thoughts for Children:

You may be adopted or may know someone who was adopted. In our verses today we read that God has adopted us. That probably sounds silly if you are already in a family. If you are in a family, you know that our families are not perfect. Moms and dads sin against children, children disobey their parents, grandparents don't always love their grandchildren the way they should. Our families aren't perfect. The only perfect Father is God and He has decided to make you His child.

He makes you His child so that you can have a relationship with Him. It is pretty neat to think that you can have the God who made the whole universe as your dad. Since God is your dad, that makes Jesus your brother! Even though right now you and I are in families that don't always love the way we should, one day we will go to our forever home. In our forever home we will love and be loved perfectly. In our forever home, Heaven, God's love will make us so lovely that we will never sin against anybody or be sinned against again. So right now, when you feel like you aren't loved by your parents, you can know that God loves you completely and fully and one day you will be home with Him.

December 13

Read: Romans 5:8

Thoughts for Parents:

Are you beginning to get a picture of how amazing God's love is for you? How can we ever relegate the thought of it to white noise or a yawn? To be loved by God is the most important thing about you. It's everything and it touches every part of who you are and how you treat others. You are loved. You can love.

Here's more: God didn't love you because He looked ahead and saw what a wonderful person you would be. No, He saw you exactly as you are and loved you anyway. That's what Romans 5:8 tells us: God demonstrates His love for us in that while we were still sinners, not great Christians He's happy to welcome…while we were sinners, Christ died for us.

Sometimes we think that God couldn't possibly love us any more because we've sinned in *that* way again. But this verse tells us that our sin never surprises God. It tells us that

He decided to love us right in the face of all our sin…while we were still in our sin, still sinners!

How often do you feel like God might sort-of-love you because He's promised to and therefore is obligated, but He also sort-of-wishes you'd be more loveable. *Oh, rejoice!* God loves you at your worst. He loved you while you were still a sinner. He is best glorified by us when we trust in His love for us and believe that He isn't lying. It is then that we will love Him and have love for our neighbor. Christ didn't die for righteous people, for those who have fulfilled all the law and been really good. No, He died for sinners, like you and me.

Thoughts for Children:

We have been talking all week about how much God loves us. That is what Christmas is all about. Today our verse tells us when God loved us. It says, "while we were still sinners." Did you hear what it said? It didn't say "while we were good boys and girls" or "while we did everything just exactly right." It said, "while we were still sinners." That means that when we were in the middle of doing something bad, God loved us.

That doesn't sound quite right, does it? We think that God only loves the good people.

The truth is that God's love is what makes good people, not that good people make God love them. Think of the worst thing you have done, maybe you hit someone, or stole something, or lied, or maybe something even worse than all of those things. In that very moment, God loved you. That is pretty hard to believe isn't it? That is why we need help to believe, we need God to convince us that His love is true and real. We need to hear every day how much He loves us. We need to hear that you can't be good enough to earn His love and you can't be bad enough for Him to stop loving you. That is what Christmas is all about: God's love coming down to earth and right at you no matter what you do.

December 14

Read: Romans 8:28-39

Thoughts for Parents:

Oh, this passage! What a glorious assurance is here for us! No matter what you are facing today, no matter how far from God's purposes and love you believe yourself to be; you have promises here that, if you take them seriously, *must* transform how you face this day.

Here they are: Because of God's great love for you everything that comes into your life today is guaranteed to be for your good and must result in the completion of God's purpose in your life--a purpose to declare you forgiven and righteous in His sight, a purpose to transform you into His Son's glorious bride.

God's will for your life is absolutely certain because if He loves you and therefore is for you, the One who gave up His Son for you will most assuredly give you all things. No one can stand against us or bring any charge against us, no matter how true that charge looks on the surface! Because

Jesus Christ has already done all the hard work, because He already died, was raised, and ascended in our place, for us, as our representative, we can be sure that He will continue to love us and intercede for us. Nothing in all creation — nothing in your own heart, your life, your family, your faith (or lack of it!) will ever be strong enough to separate you from God's love for you in Christ.

Thoughts for Children:

Have you ever felt like no one was on your side? Have you ever felt like your day couldn't get any worse, like everything in the whole world was going wrong? Have you ever felt like nobody loved you? If you have felt that way I have some exciting news for you. Our verses today take every single one of those thoughts and they turn them right around. When you feel like no one is on your side, you can remember that God says He is for us. He is on your side. When you feel like your day is awful and everything is wrong, you can remember that

God promises that everything in your life works together for good, even all the bad stuff He takes and uses to make good things. When you feel like nobody loves you, or nobody should love you because you are bad, you can remember that God promises that nothing, absolutely nothing can change His great love for you. That makes me want to jump up and down and do a happy dance, what about you?

Activity Time

Week two: Love

For this week's activity, we remember that God is our refuge.

Grab cushions, blankets, sheets, pillows, and all your live/stuffed animals to make a giant fort in the living room!

If you're feeling especially zealous, create a bin with all the ingredients for a fort: clothespins, flashlights, sheets (as an award winning fort builder, these are better than heavy blankets), stuff for s'mores, and some fun Christmas books you checked out from the library earlier that day because you're amazing (or, if you're me, the three books already laying on the floor from earlier that afternoon which have nothing to do with Christmas).

If you don't have a fire pit readily available (or don't want to burn your house down) to cook your s'mores, simply put graham crackers out on a foiled sheet pan.

Then, add a piece of chocolate and a large marshmallow on top, then bake at 350 degrees for 5 minutes. When you take them out, smash it down with another graham cracker and commence gaining 5 lbs.

Some questions to ponder, if you aren't too busy stuffing your faces:

1. What do you think it means that God is our refuge?

2. When is it easier to rest? When you know that you are protected or when you are afraid that something bad is going to happen?

Link this activity to the fact that God is in charge and is our protector and refuge in all of life; even when things seem really scary, we are hidden in Him-just like we are hidden under all these blankets. We can rest when we know and believe this fact about God. Remember that last week we learned that God is trustworthy and does not lie.

December 15

Light the third candle (pink; the Shepherd's Candle), which represents joy.

Read: Psalm 92 , Luke 2:8-20

Thoughts for Parents:

This week we will be focusing in on joy, the joy of the Psalmist as he considers God's work and the joy of the shepherds at the news that they had been privy to see the One who would be the Messiah.

Surely these shepherds were men who had heard from their youth about the promised One to come. Perhaps they still believed it — perhaps not. Perhaps they were like most of us, believing-sort-of, when they thought of it, when they remembered. Sure, they had recited Psalm 92 on the Sabbath, they knew it was good "to give thanks to the Lord," to sing praises to His name in the morning and at night. Sure, they were thankful for God's creation, and yes, there had been times when they watched the lambs or looked out on a night sky glutted with stars and a song of joy sprang from their hearts. But, let's face it: life as a shepherd wasn't easy, and the nights were cold and dark, the wolves were dangerous, thieves were cunning, the sheep were stupid, and the ground was hard. Then God changed everything. The light of the stars was eclipsed by the glory of the Lord. An angel spoke to them: Don't be afraid! Good news! Great joy was being proclaimed—joy even for lowly shepherds!

What was this good news? Where would this great joy come from? Had Herod finally been deposed? Had the Romans packed it in at last? Was a mighty conqueror finally taking note of their plight? Well, yes and no. Yes a new King who would deliver them from their enemies had come, but not quite in the way they might have expected. What was the sign of this new kingdom, this great good news? Look for an infant wrapped in rags lying in a feeding trough in a barn.

Wait…what? A baby? Born in a barn? Uncouthness, coarseness, rudeness exemplified. Weakness incarnate. Poverty and want wrapped up in rags. Why? Why had God done this? So that we could rejoice in our salvation. This i nfant still damp from the womb He had gestated in is the Savior — the Savior of the uncouth, coarse, rude and poor. He's the Savior of sinners who are too lazy or absent-minded to close a door. Rejoice.

Thoughts for children:

This whole week we are going to be talking about joy. Joy is what you feel on Christmas morning when you get to open your presents. The joy that we are going to talk about doesn't end. We wake up with joy on Christmas morning because we are looking forward to what we might get, but sometimes we don't get exactly what we asked for or our toys break and then our joy ends. The great thing about the joy we are going to talk about all week is it never ends, because our joy is Jesus.

Can you imagine the joy that the shepherds must have felt when they saw all those angels? Think of it, pretend like you were one of those shepherds, there you are minding your own business, sleeping, maybe even having a good dream, and then, "BAM!" All of sudden, the sky is filled with angels and they are all singing a song that makes you so happy! You know why the song they sang made them happy? Because it promised that God would be at peace with all those who love Him. Peace with God means we are His friends, we are in His family, and He loves us. That should make you happy, too! The angels told the shepherds that Jesus was being born. That is the how we have peace with God. Jesus made it so we could have a relationship with God. That is the good news that should always bring a smile to your face.

December 16

Read: Isa 35:1-10

Thoughts for Parents:

I'm in the mood for some good news. Aren't you? My life isn't really any different from yours. I have to get up in the morning and try to figure out how I'm going to get all the stuff done that I need to get done with what I have at hand. I have to figure out how to care for my husband, my kids, their kids, my aging mother, my friends and the folks in the church who need me. I have to figure out how to do the work God's given me to do. Then I look around at my resources and I see just what you see when you look at your resources: There never seems to be enough of the right stuff to accomplish the work I need to do. And then, of course, there's the problem of my sin. I simply don't know how I'm going to have the wherewithal to do what I need to do when I need to do it. I need some good news.

Here it is: The good news is that for those who trust in the Savior, an everlasting joy is promised. A day is coming when there will be more than enough of everything and all my desires for sin will have been transformed into love for Him. I'll see the burning sands of this sin-riddled world transformed into cleansing, life-giving pools; I'll watch the "thirsty ground" change into springs of water. All the places where dangerous adversaries used to find shelter will be transformed into the river of God's delights (Psalm 36:8). This is God's doing!

How will this happen? How will we get to this oasis? Our Savior, Jesus the God-Man, has paved the way on this Highway of Holiness. He cut the road out of the rocky ground; He covered it with the stones of His good works, cementing them together with His blood. He's made it all the way past Calvary, that haunt of jackals, and paved the road right into the throne room of God for us.

I love how the ESV translates verse 8b, "It shall belong to those who walk on the way; even if they are fools, they shall not go astray."

Okay, that means I qualify. It means that even in my foolishness, weakness and sin, I and all who believe will finally and, at last, find the gladness and joy that had always been out of reach.

Thoughts for Children:

Have you ever wanted a special something so badly that it is all you ever think about? I am sure that right now you have a few things in mind that you really, really want for Christmas. Have you ever gotten a present that you had been asking and asking for? Remember how good it felt to open that present, tear apart the wrapping paper and see the very thing you wanted inside the box? Remember how happy that gift made you? Funny thing is that happiness goes away. Maybe it takes a week, or a day, or maybe even just an hour, but all of a sudden you want something else to make you happy. Do you know why you feel that way? Because God made you so that nothing would really make you happy but Him. Our hearts are only meant to be completely joyful because of Him. He is the only thing big enough to make us forever happy.

While we are here on earth we still have to try and remember this truth. We forget that God is our happiness. But one day, "unending joy will crown us, happiness and joy will overwhelm us." When we get to heaven nothing will be able to take away the joy that is our crown. Happiness and joy will be all we know. Every time you feel sadness you can remember this, one day all the sadness will be gone and we will only have smiles forever.

December 17

Read: Matthew 11:2-10

Thoughts for Parents:

I'll admit it: sometimes I rejoice about the wrong things. Sometimes I smirk with glee when some ne'er-do-well gets his comeuppance. Even though I really love to think and talk about grace, I'm really a legalist at heart. I want certain people to get what they deserve. Not me, of course. That's not what I want. I want mercy...but there are just other folks who I think deserve a swift kick. In this respect, I don't think my thinking is that far from John the Baptizer's.

John had been imprisoned for telling Herod the truth about his unlawful "marriage" and while he rotted there, awaiting execution for standing against the sins of his culture, he heard that Jesus was healing the blind, the lame, lepers, and the deaf. He heard that the dead were being raised up. And he heard that Jesus was preaching a message of good news. Good news? Yes, good news and he was preaching it to sinners! But, what about the message of repentance? Shouldn't Jesus be focusing on what these people needed to *do*? Shouldn't he be calling down fire upon them for their unbelief and idolatry?

John's perspective on what should be preached to whom was being shattered by Christ's great love and condescension to sinners. Jesus offended John. Why? Because Jesus was hanging out with prostitutes and tax-collectors (aka crack-ho's and mafia). Yes, He was standing against the religious establishment but He wasn't worried about being the morality police. He crushed the people by telling them they needed to be perfect and then He gave them good news: Perfection was here, in the flesh. This was the news that John and the rest of us needed to hear and yet hated to hear.

Here's the bottom line: The only way to find joy in Christ's work on our behalf is to stop being offended by grace. Grace is promiscuous. It's utterly ridiculous. It's unruly; because of it, those nasty folks who should get a whack get a blessing instead. Of course, once you realize that you fall into the "nasty folk" category, you'll be more comfortable about grace. Happy is the one who is not offended by Jesus.

Thoughts for Children:

How would you feel if you had been blind your whole life and then suddenly you could see? Or what about if you couldn't walk and then all of a sudden you could do flips and run? Or if you couldn't hear a single thing and then your ears worked wonderfully? Or if you had a terrible problem with your skin and then all of a sudden you were healed? Or what about if you were dead, and then all of a sudden you were alive again? I bet that would make you so happy, so full of joy.

Well here is some crazy news for you; the Bible says that we are dead because of our sins. Not actually dead, but as far as God was concerned you were dead. You still might be dead to God because of your sins. You are probably wondering how to become alive to God.

All you have to do is believe, believe that all Jesus came to live the life you couldn't live. You see God tells us we have to be perfect, we can't do that, so Jesus came and did that for us. He also came and took all the punishment for your sin. So, because of Jesus' work, we are alive to God. Jesus did all the hard work. He makes us alive. We just believe. We can smile all day today knowing that we were once dead and now we are alive.

December 18

Read: Psalm 20

Thoughts for Parents:

If all you knew about Christianity was the story of Calvary, you wouldn't think that it was very good news. If the message ended with, "And Jesus uttered a loud cry and breathed his last" (Mark 15:37), you wouldn't really have heard anything worth rejoicing over. What's there to rejoice about in a beaten, shamed Man, hanging in death on a Roman pike? Why would you sing praises then? The crucifixion only becomes good news when it is seen from the vantage point of the resurrection.

Psalm 20 tells us that the key to our salvation is bound up with the salvation of the King, the Christ, whose very title means "anointed one." If, and only if, the Anointed King Jesus is delivered from defeat, is our deliverance secured. And yet, what do we see on that dark mount? Do we see Him being delivered on Calvary? No...not at all. What we see is the theoretical triumph of evil and the final humiliation of a Man of uncertain lineage who seemed like a good idea that has proven defective at the last.

David was sure that "the Lord saves his anointed;" that he would "answer Him from his holy heaven with the saving might of his right hand" (Psalm 20:6). He was sure that when the anointed called out, the Lord in heaven would answer. But that's not what happened on Calvary. No, in fact, we see just the opposite. The Anointed King calls out and isn't answered. He isn't delivered…and all our hope for deliverance and salvation is in vain. Until the resurrection, that is.

It is in the resurrection that everything we hope for is finally secured. The resurrection assures us that Christ's offering of perfect obedience and propitiatory sacrifice has been accepted on our behalf. The resurrection is God's final (and life-giving) shout of "AMEN!" to Jesus' faithful, "It is finished." Because He has been delivered, because He has arisen and stood upright, we know that we will too.

We can be sure now that God will send us help and support when we call. We can rejoice that He will grant us our godly desires and forgive and love us. And so, in response, we, too, can shout for joy. Does the Lord save His anointed ones? Does He rescue those who don't trust in their own goodness and strength but rather in the goodness and strength of Christ? Yes! So we respond, "O Lord, you have saved the King! And because of that we can rejoice in knowing that you will answer us when we call."

Thoughts for Children:

Do you ever wonder if God hears you when you pray? I know sometimes it feels like I am just talking to nobody. Our verses today tell us something very different. Our verse tells us that God does hear us, and He does answer us when we pray. The really good news is that He doesn't hear and answer us when we pray because we are good little boys and girls. God knows

all that is in your heart and every thing you think and He knows that you are not a good little boy or girl. Now that might not sound like very good news to you, that might not make you smile. If my friends knew all of my thoughts, I am pretty sure I wouldn't have any friends any more. They would see how selfish am and always wanted the good things that they had. They would see how angry I get when I don't get my way. God knows those things about us, but He doesn't see them anymore. How is that possible? Because we are hiding in Jesus. When God looks at us, all He sees is His perfect Son who did everything right all the time.

Because Jesus was born, because of how he lived, and because died for us, we can know that God will always hear our prayers and always answer us, one more reason to smile today.

December 19

Read: Hebrews 12:1-2, 12

Thoughts for Parents:

Jesus was joyful. In fact, Hebrews 1:9 says that because He loved righteousness and hated wickedness, His Father had caused Him to be gladder than anyone around Him. Jesus knew what it was to laugh a belly laugh, to smile, to have joy. You wouldn't have thought of Him as grumpy or a stick in the mud. He was fun to be around. Of course, that doesn't mean that He was superficial or silly or that He told off-color jokes, or that He wasn't serious when humor wasn't appropriate. Unlike us, He knew how to be happy without sinning. But Jesus also knew what it was to suffer. During His entire life as a weak man and especially during His last few hours, He was sustained by looking forward to promised bliss. He looked forward to "the joy that was set before him" as He endured the cross, thinking nothing of the shame that probably would have stopped most of us. *Be treated like that? Not hardly!* His hope of a future joy was strongly tethered to the truth that a day was coming when He would sit again at the right hand of His Father's throne—but this time He would be bearing the flesh He'd been given in Mary's little womb. He'd gone away as the Word, the Second Person of the Trinity; He would return as the God-Man, Jesus, the Christ, forever outfitted in His wedding garb, our flesh.

You know, it's easy for us to think that Jesus' faith-walk was effortless; after all, He was God. But nothing could be farther from the truth. The entire time He lived here, He never accessed His deity in order to make obedience, faith, or life easier for himself. He lived just like you and I do, walking by faith and not by sight. He believed that His Father would welcome Him to heaven, although He had been forever transformed from God, the Word, to Jesus, the God-Man. He believed that His bride would love Him. So, it was in the light of this great hope that He persevered through the deepest pit of suffering: His Father's forsaking Him and pouring out His entire wrath for all our sin on His head. He kept His eye fixed on the joy of relationship and reunion with His Father and with us.

Now, if that doesn't produce joy in your heart, I simply don't know what will. He ran the race with patience that was set before Him so that He would be able to perfectly represent us: as the obedient Son, the slaughtered Lamb, the risen King.

Thoughts for Children:

Today we hear about how happy Jesus was. Now you might think that He was only happy when good things happened, I know that's when I'm happy. But our verse says that Jesus was thinking about joy when He went to the cross. It was actually what helped Him go through the hardest, most painful, worst thing in His entire life. The thought of making you one of His brothers or sisters, the thought of making you one of God's kids, the thought of all of us being together someday with Him in Heaven, these were the thoughts that helped Him get through the most difficult thing He ever had to do.

When you have days that are hard, where nothing seems to be going right, and nothing makes you smile, remember Jesus: He loves you right in the middle of your frown. Thinking of Him will help you smile, it makes us strong. Thinking about His love for us will be what helps you get through those really tough, nothing is going right days. His love is just that great and just that good.

December 20

Read: Rev. 21:4

Thoughts for Parents:

Truthfully, there are days when it seems like crying, death, mourning and pain will never end. Of course, by His grace not every day is a day of overwhelming sorrow. However, there are enough of these days now for me to long for the time when laughter, life, joy, and vitality are mine. Forever.

The Apostle John brought us this vision of a new day. He was given a taste of future glory, and, like us, He needed it. John was living in exile, away from his home, his friends, and his church. It would have been easy for him to have been discouraged--it wasn't good for him to be alone and there was nothing he could do to change it. His aloneness was being enforced by the Roman emperor, Domitian. So the Lord Jesus, out of great love for His best friend, visited him (not even Domitian could keep King Jesus away from His friends) and brought him some good news. Yes, things looked really terrible. Yes, Domitian's power seemed limitless, and he certainly could make John's life miserable, but this life was not all the life that John had. His life was hidden with Christ in heaven. Like John, we need to be reminded that there is a loving King who is overseeing everything and no power is able to stop King Jesus from visiting us and bringing us to Himself in great joy.

Earthly powers had tried to stop Jesus before. Herod had all the babies in Bethlehem slaughtered. Women wept in great mourning, but Jesus was safe. His mission to overcome all our sorrow, all our exile and isolation wouldn't, *couldn't* be thwarted. And even though we're physically separated from him right now, a day will surely come when we will finally be home, a day when "the dwelling place of God" will be with man. "He will dwell with them, and they will be his people, and God himself will be with them as their God. He will wipe away every tear from their eyes, and death shall be no more, neither shall here be mourning, nor crying, nor pain anymore, for the former things have passed away." Being with him in unmitigated fellowship is the answer to all our sorrow, pain, and tears.

Thoughts for Children:

You know how good it feels to come home sometimes? Like when you have been away from your parents and you get home and there are chocolate chips cookies waiting for you? Or when it is rainy and cold outside and you run into your house and there is a nice warm fire burning in the fire place? Maybe you don't have a fireplace or warm cookies but you know how nice it is to get a hug when you walk in your door. Well that snuggly feeling of being home is only a small taste of what it is going to be like when we get to heaven.

Home should feel safe, I know sometimes it doesn't, God promises to make all the hurt and sadness in our lives become happiness some day. This should make your heart be excited about heaven. Some day we are going to have a forever home where we never cry, we never feel any pain, no one will ever die. In our forever home the most exciting thing will be that we get to be with God. He will be right there with us, and all of the times when you felt like you were praying to nothing, all of the times that you felt like no one cared, all of the times you felt alone will be gone forever. God's love will erase all of those thoughts from our memory, wipe away all of our tears and fear, and all we will know is His good smile on us for all of eternity.

December 21

Read: Nehemiah 8:10

Thoughts for Parents:

As punishment for the nation's incessant unbelief and idolatry, Israel had been captured and forced into slavery in Persia. After many years, in God's kindness, some of the exiles were allowed to return to their homeland, to rebuild the walls of Jerusalem and restore the temple.

On one certain day, Ezra read the Book of the Law of Moses to all the people...and when the people heard the Law and understood what it meant, they mourned. The Levites helped them understand the commands of the Law and as God gave them understanding, they knew they were in trouble. Imagine what it would have been like to be taken away from your home for disobedience, then to have an opportunity to return and work to rebuild your nation, only to discover that the disobedience that had eventuated in your slavery was still ongoing. The people wept. They were afraid. They knew that the judgment that had befallen their fathers was hanging over their heads as well.

As the people wept, Nehemiah, the governor, and Ezra, the priest, gave the people an astonishing command. Rather than pile on more and more law to try to get them to really repent, they told the people not to mourn or weep, "for this day is holy to the Lord your God." In fact, not only did they tell them to stop weeping, they were commanded to have a party: eat savory meat, drink sweet wine, and invite your neighbors and those who don't have a place to party. Enjoy yourself and rejoice in God's amazing generosity.

Why command them to party? Why wouldn't their leaders tell them to mourn? Because they knew that God is best glorified in hearts that are joyful. In fact, they knew that the strength they needed to begin to obey and to rebuild was a by-product of joy.

God isn't impressed by our weeping. In fact, when we know He's near it's time to remember His great kindness and rejoice. And it's only there, in that rejoicing over His love and kindness that we'll find the strength to persevere even here, even in the middle of our sorrow. That's what Christmas tells us and why we should celebrate. Yes, of course, we've broken the Law, but He's come to us to be all that we need: a Redeemer, a Perfect Representative, a dear Husband.

Thoughts for Children:

Have you ever been caught doing something really bad? I mean really, really bad. During those times where you know that what you have done is wrong, how do you feel? Are you happy and wanting to have a big party or are you sad and feeling like you want to hide under the covers? In our verse today, the people had been caught doing something very bad. You see, if we are honest, any time we look at the what the Bible tells us to do we should always feel sad because we can never do all that the Bible asks us to do. You would think that what God would want is for us to cry lots and lots when we see how bad we are. Instead, God tells us some good news; He tells us once we see how bad we are we stop crying and can go have a big party. Now that doesn't make very much sense does it? Because, if we are thinking about what we have done, we know we should feel sad, but God wants us to think about what Jesus has done. He did everything perfectly. We can be happy and throw a big party because Jesus did all the hard things for us. We can have joy even when we mess everything up, because God forgives all of our sins.

Activity Time

Week three: Joy

The shepherds were so full of joy, they couldn't contain their excitement. They HAD to tell everyone the good news!

For this week's activity, we're going use newspaper to make an ornament. This ornament will help us remember Christ as the good news when we see it hanging on the tree.

There are lots of different options for ornaments. The first option is:

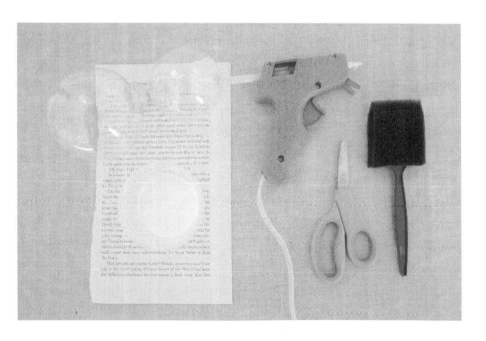

You can simply use a ball ornament that you already have and glue pieces of newspaper onto it. (I recommend using a crafting glue like Mod-Podge.) There need be no particular shape to the pieces; random is fine. After you create your pieces of paper, brush the glue on the ball, then put the pieces of paper on the ball. Smooth it as much as you can.

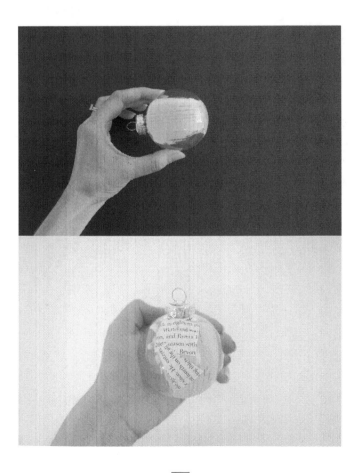

When the whole ball is covered with paper, paint the entire ball with a light covering of the glue to seal it. If you have very little ones, you might not seal it until they go to bed to save yourself from sprouting 4 to 5 new grey hairs …

The second option is:

If you want to get a little more elaborate, you can cut the paper into uniform, dime-sized circles and layer them with hot glue in rows until the ornament is completely covered.

You can do one ornament or 20! It's up to your crafterdark ability to stay awake or handle children with glue.

While you are working on these activities you can ask these questions:

1) Can you think of a time you were so excited about something that you just felt like you would explode if you didn't tell someone?

2) Can you think of a time when you had waited and waited for something and it finally happened?

You can link this to God's promise that He would send His son to save the world. God's people had been waiting for a very long time for him, and then all of a sudden, Jesus had FINALLY arrived! Remember these last few weeks, we've learned that God keeps His promises and we can rest knowing that He is in control, even when we have to wait.

December 22

Light the final purple candle (the Angels' Candle), which represents peace.

Read: Psalm 85

Thoughts for Parents:

In Psalm 85, we find ourselves, once again, with the people of Israel who are lamenting over their sin and hoping that God will show them favor, once again. How can God's peace, His *shalom* be with them and with us, when we know that we have failed in so many ways? How dare we approach Him in the hope of being forgiven and blessed rather than judged and cursed?

When the Bible speaks of God being at peace with us, it is not necessarily a *feeling* of peacefulness that is being referenced. Instead, it is a cessation of hostilities; in this case, it is God who is the offended party who has the right and authority to be angry with us, whose hot wrath has been completely satisfied so that He can be both "just and the justifier." Don't misunderstand: It's not that God just decides to overlook our little tiny mistakes. No, we have done more than make a little tiny mistake. We've been in rebellion against His Word and way our entire life; yet, here we are hoping for forgiveness, reconciliation, and peace. It would be audacious if we weren't commanded to hope in this way.

What is our only hope? Our only hope lies in His character, where steadfast love and faithfulness meet. He is righteous enough, good enough, and consistent enough to always keep all His promises, and He has promised that no one who calls on Him will ever be cast aside (Romans 10:13). Our peace with God does not rest on our own ability to be in complete compliance with His commands at all times. No, our peace with God rests in that little baby crying in His cold manger. He's the One who has steadfast love, faithfulness and righteousness and it's in His Person, weak though it seems. That peace is brought to us through one kiss of grace from the Father to His rebel creation.

Thoughts for Children:

It is Christmas week! We have been waiting for this week all year long. It is going to be hard to remember the real reason we celebrate Christmas when we are so excited about presents. So, let's take a few minutes today and remember what our real Present is, the only Present that will make us really happy. This week we are going to talk about peace. Peace with God is knowing in your deepest down part of your heart that God is not mad at you and that all He feels is love for you, His child. We have talked about it a lot this past month, but do you remember why God isn't mad at you? It is only because of Jesus, because of the baby that was born thousands of years ago in Bethlehem. God's love for you will never end because of Jesus. God's love for you is steadfast, that is a fancy way of saying no matter what you do His love stays the same. His love is always there. His love forgives every wrong thing that we have done in the past, all the wrong things we do today, and every wrong thing that you will do in the future. Jesus dying on the cross took away all of God's anger for *all* the wrong things you have done; this is peace. God will always give us what is good for us and is never mad at us--that is the peace that we have with Him, that is part of our incredible present that we get not only on Christmas day, but every day.

December 23

Read: Isaiah 52:7, 53:5

Thoughts for Parents:

Everyone is longing for a message of peace, of good news, and of happiness. We're longing to know that we've been saved and that salvation is more than something hoped for at Christmas, but is actually ours. What do I want for Christmas? I want to know that God is no longer angry with me and that I've been saved by His grace.

But how can this happen? How can salvation be ours? It is only ours only because God is in charge. If it were up to us to procure our own salvation, if we had to save up enough good works to finally merit it, we would be lost. It is only through the good news of peace between God and man proclaimed, "Your God reigns!"

Why is that such good news? It's good news because it means that the God who created us, who saw our fall, who knows our sin, unbelief, and idolatry implicitly and yet loves us, is in charge. He's in charge of our salvation and that, my friends, is really great news. It is only through one glad declaration, "Your God reigns!" that we find ultimate assurance knowing that He is completely at peace with us.

But this end of hostilities between God and man didn't happen without great cost to Him. Someone needed to bear the "chastisement" due us. Someone needed to be pierced and crushed and wounded so that we could be called sons and daughters rather than enemies and rebels. Someone had to bring both God and man together into one...and that One is nursing at His mother's breast, wrapped in rags.

God is at peace with us and that's the happiest news we've ever been given. What are you hoping for this Christmas? For a new something, or for the family to get together and enjoy one another, or that you'll have just enough of everything that no one will feel left out or disappointed? Are you hoping that a particular relative will finally stop fussing with you?

All those lesser blessings are fine, but the one blessing we all need is this: God is in charge and He's done everything necessary for us to be completely reconciled to Him. Happy news!

Thoughts for Children:

What are you hoping for this week? Are you hoping for lots of fun parties and yummy food and awesome presents? Those things are all good gifts from God and they all cost something. Someone had to pay for the food, and for the presents, and for the gas to get to the party, and for the car that you rode in to the party, and for the clothes you will wear to the party, and...well, you understand what I'm saying. Most good things cost something. Our best thing cost Jesus everything. Peace with God--knowing that God isn't mad at us--cost Jesus and God their hearts. God loved Jesus with everything and He had to give Him up so that Jesus could die for our sins. Jesus had to give His life. Jesus had to take all the punishment for our sins so that we could know for sure God wasn't mad at us.

So, while you open your gifts, and have fun at your parties, and eat your yummy food, remember the cost.

Remember that Jesus loved you with His whole life. Remember that nothing will ever be able to make Him stop loving you. Remember that it cost Him everything to make you and God have a relationship. Remember that the relationship with God is a forever gift; no one can take it away. What good news that makes us smile!

Activity Time

Week four: Peace

This week we learned about the angels singing for joy at the coming of baby Jesus. There was a lot of literal rejoicing and singing!

For this week's activity, it's time to brush off those vocal cords and do some caroling. Right now, many of you are deciding not to do this activity, but bear with me! If you're too embarrassed to go from neighbor to neighbor singing, perhaps drive to a friend's house or to the grandparents and surprise them with *Joy to the World*. Force them to make you desert, or bring it with you and force them to eat it with you. That's incredibly motivating even for the shyest of the shy.

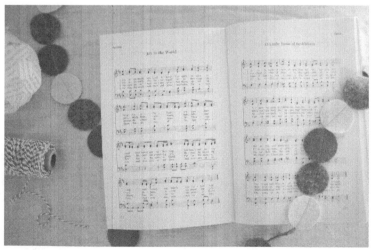

If caroling is an absolute no-go for you, consider pulling out the boombox...errr ipod...and sing along to carols together as a family. Christmas Carols, like *Joy to the World* and *Angels We Have Heard on High*, are fraught with incredible theology. But sometimes, when we hear them over and over at Christmas time, they seem more sentimental than deeply theological and cease to bring us to ponder the amazing gift of Jesus. Help your children to learn to hear these songs for more than sentiment by picking out a phrase or two in the songs and discussing them (you can find lyrics for any song on the web, if you need or want to). For example, ask, "What do you think *joy to the world* really means?" or "Why do you think there was such a big concert in the sky?"

Just like worship time in church, singing is another way to help remind us who God is. If you were an angel singing in the sky, what do you think you would be singing about God? **You can link this back to all the traits we've learned about Him these past few weeks.**

- God is faithful and keeps his promises.

- God is in control and we can reset knowing and believing that.

- God is good news to the world. He is our Savior!

- And this week, God is worthy of all of our praise.

December 24

Light the Christmas Candle (White)

Read: Luke 2:14

Thoughts for Parents:

Angels had watched in awe as the Son, the second person of the Trinity, the Word, entered into an ovum of a young girl. They had wondered as their Beloved took to himself human flesh and blood, formed a brain, grew fingernails, received nourishment through an umbilical cord. They knew He was changing, growing, and their joy that God's creation would soon get to see Him was limitless. They waited while His mother labored in pain and marveled in wonder when they saw His face...it was a human face now. When He took a breath, everything on this dark planet changed.

"Glory to God in the highest!" they shouted. "There will be peace now on earth! He's coming to those with whom He is pleased!" God alone is wise enough to formulate a plan to save this cursed world. God alone loves enough to send His most treasured Son to be part of it. God alone is powerful enough to cause it to come about, just as He had foretold, and just at the right moment. And, God alone is good enough to continue to love when even His chosen ones had turned from Him…and will continue to turn from Him.

It is interesting that the angels sang songs about peace at this moment because Jesus himself said that He didn't come to bring peace but rather a sword (Matthew 10:34). Within a few months, a sword will find its way to Bethlehem, a sword that will deprive infants and toddlers of life. Jesus himself knew better than anyone else that love for Him might bring conflict in families — but in comparison to the assurance of peace with God, conflict with others is miniscule. Everywhere Jesus went, He had a polarizing affect; He was the sort of Man you either loved or hated because He was so very consistently himself.

Tonight, we can glorify God because He's sent His Son to bring peace for His loved ones between heaven and earth. Yes, there is and always will be wars and rumors of wars here.

Soon the kingdom of peace that He has promised will be fully realized and all the sin that produces all our conflicts will be gone and we will be able to rest fully in Him. "Glory to God in the highest!"

Thoughts for Children:

It is Christmas Eve!! Tomorrow is the big day! Perhaps in your family you open all of your presents today, and so right now you are wishing you could just go and play. When you opened your favorite gift or when you open your best gift tomorrow you are going to feel very excited. You might even say, "Yippeeee!!!!" You might even do a little dance. That feeling of excitement you will have is how the angels felt when they came to tell the shepherds the good news. The shouted, "GLORY!!!!" That is another way to say, "YIPPEEEE!!! THE MOST EXCITING THING HAS HAPPENED!!!!"

Do you know why they shouted "Glory to God?" Well, it was because they knew that Jesus was coming to make peace between God and us. They knew what Jesus being born would do for our lives. They knew how Jesus would change everything for us. The angels knew the good news. Do you know the good news? Do you know that Jesus lived the life that we are supposed to live, that He always obeyed? Do you know that Jesus took all of the punishment that we deserve for all of our sin? Do you know that right now, when He looks at you, God sees Jesus? I hope you know all of those happy things, because that is what we have been talking about for the whole month. We can shout, "GLORY TO GOD!", just like the angels did way back then, because we know now the good news they knew that day in Bethlehem.

December 25

Read: John 14:27

Thoughts for Parents:

We've counted the days. We've lit the candles. And now we're ready to celebrate. We're celebrating family and friends and one another with gifts and lights. It's Christmas Day! He's finally arrived! And with Him He's brought us hope, love, joy, and peace. The day is finally here and He brings us a word of comfort:

Peace I leave with you; my peace I give to you. Not as the world gives do I give to you. Let not your hearts be troubled, neither let them be afraid.

Today you're probably going to spend some time in giving and receiving. Our family all joins together and we're going to give gifts and eat together and rejoice. And as wonderful as we anticipate this day will be, it will still be "as the world gives."

How does the world give? The world gives in response

to what it has been given. It's the principle of karma: what goes around comes around. The world gives better gifts to those who have the ability to repay in kind; the world gives the best gifts to those who deserve them. But Jesus' gift of peace isn't like that. Jesus' gift of peace isn't in response to our deserving. No, in fact, He gives peace to those who deserve judgment. He gives the gift of well-being, blessedness, peace, *shalom,* out of the boundless sea of His grace.

In addition, His gift of peace will never fade away. We may; indeed, get the gift we're hoping for…but let's face it, after a time that gift will fade away. It will either fade away because it's last year's cell phone and it's lost its cutting edge or it will fade away because our fickle hearts will have moved on to something else all too soon. But the gift that our Savior gives, the gift of peace with Him will never fade. In other words, we'll never wear out our welcome at His Father's throne and hearing this great story will never get old. We are at peace with Him.

So...Merry Christmas! Love and enjoy this day and all that it means. St the end of the day, when you see that perhaps you could have done something better, remember that He's completely satisfied and at peace with you.

Thoughts for Children:

IT IS CHRISTMAS DAY! We can shout, "Merry Christmas!" all day long. Today is the day that our sweet Savior, Jesus Christ, was born. Today is the day that He started His life here on earth, the day that He was sent to make peace between us and God, the day that He started breathing in order for us to be sure that God loves us forever, the day that He blinked His eyes for the first time so that we could have happiness and joy forever, the day that He cried His first cry so that we could know we will always have hope.

Today is the day that we can celebrate what Christmas is really all about: Jesus. Christmas is about Him, and--let me tell you a little secret--*every* day of *every* year is about Him, too. It is about the truth that He will never ever leave us...no mater what. He gives us peace, He gives us joy, He gives us

hope, and He gives us His love forever. So, enjoy your day,

have fun, laugh, eat, be happy, and celebrate Jesus!

---

[i] Many of the reading choices are taken from the Revised Common Lectionary Daily Reading or The Book of Common
[ii] Unless otherwise noted, all Scripture quotations are taken from The Holy Bible, English Standard Version® (ESV®), copyright © 2001 by Crossway, a publishing ministry of Good News Publishers. Used by permission. All rights reserved.
[iii] *My Blue Heaven,* Hawn/Sylbert Movie Company and Warner Brothers, Burbank, California, 1990.

Made in the USA
Lexington, KY
13 November 2013